SOUTH WESTERN APPROACHES

Air Operations from Pembrokeshire in the World Wars

Wg. Cdr. J. E. Tipton, D.F.C.
(Hon. Curator, Tenby Museum)

ISBN 0 904696 04 9

Tenby Museum   1986

First Published 1986
Reprinted 1991

Printed by Tredeml Print
Narberth, Pembrokeshire, Dyfed

Contents

I	**Introduction**		4
II	**The Great War**		5
II	**Between the Wars**		7
IV	**War Operations**		11
	1.	The Opening Shots	11
	2.	To the End of 1940	12
	3.	1941	16
	4.	1942	19
	5.	Fighter Defence	22
	6.	1943	25
	7.	Ground Radar	32
	8.	1944	33
	9.	1945 and the End	36
V	**Coastal Command Non-Operational Units**		37
	1.	Haverfordwest and Templeton	37
	2.	Coastal Command Development Unit	38
	3.	No. 4 Armament Practice Camp	39
	4.	Non-Operational Flying Boat Units	39
VI	**Units Outside Coastal Command**		40
	1.	Anti-Aircraft Co-operation - RAF	40
	2.	Naval Land Based Flying Units	41
	3.	Carew Cheriton as a Training Station	41
	4.	Rudbaxton	41
	5.	Ferry Training	42
	6.	Transport Conversion	43
VII	**Conclusion**		43

SOUTH WESTERN APPROACHES

Air Operations from Pembrokeshire in the World Wars

I

A military establishment is like an island in the civilian community, surrounded by physical and intelligence security and engaged in activities very different from the life around it. In normal times this isolation is partly bridged by social life, service families and the traffic of civilian workers; in war, however, particularly in the case of air bases, those within the perimeter may be engaged at the sharpest end of the fighting while outside the gates life is more or less normal, and communication between the two worlds is reduced to guarded conversation in the welfare canteen and the pub.

Once the war is over, the strangers disperse and the account of what they were doing disappears into archives for the next thirty years, after which it can be extracted only with some difficulty. Nevertheless the air operations of the world wars are important chapters in local, as well as in national, history and those of Pembrokeshire no less important than of the counties facing the continent.

Pembrokeshire commands the south-western approaches and Milford Haven is a focal point for shipping. This was recognised very early in the evolution of military aviation, hydroplane tests taking place at Dale in 1912. These were not very successful, but in the following year land for a hangar was acquired and one of the dockyard slipways was made available for the assembly of seaplanes; the first sight of a flying machine over Milford was in October 1913. The plan to establish a base came however to nothing, and aircraft were not used to cover the sea routes through the area until 1916.

By the Second World War maritime reconnaissance aircraft were able to operate well out into the Atlantic and around the approaches to the enemy harbours. The changing fortunes of the war were directly reflected in the activities of the Pembrokeshire bases from September 1939 until victory in Europe. The distance from the main areas of enemy air cover made the county equally suitable for non-operational flying to take place reasonably free from disturbance.

II - THE GREAT WAR

Pembrokeshire was important to war at sea long before the development of aircraft, Milford Haven being a vital point in the circulation of both merchant and naval shipping. The protection of shipping visiting and passing through the area became increasingly of concern during the Great War as the numbers and the efficiency of enemy submarines increased.

In February 1915 the Germans embarked on a campaign of unrestricted submarine warfare, any ship within the war zone being liable to attack. Shipping losses rose to over one hundred thousand tons a month. The value of air patrols in keeping submarines submerged, if not in sinking them, was now recognised. It was to extend air cover to the south west approaches that in August 1915 the Admiralty acquired 228 acres of land at Sageston. Two sheds of corrugated iron were erected, large enough to house airships and by early 1916 the Royal Naval Air Station, Pembroke (as it was known) was ready to provide 'aviation facilities'. The first ascent was made on 25 April with Commander Fuller as Observer and Midshipman Colson as the pilot.

The airships were non-rigid 'blimps', the earliest being classified SS, for 'Submarine Search', followed by the larger C, 'Coastal' types. RNAS Pembroke was equipped with SS 14A, SS 40, SS 42A, SS Z and C 3 machines at different times. For communication they carried a wireless telegraph with a range, in favourable conditions, of up to 100 miles. At first they patrolled the shipping lanes but after May 1917, when the convoy system was introduced, their main task became the escort of these groups of vessels. It was in this role that they were most effective.

In the following year the operation of airplanes was added, the first flight from the airfield being made by Sub-Lieutenant Allaway on 29 April 1917. They were Sopwith 1½ Strutters, four at first, reinforced by a further four at the end of June. They were housed in a hangar at the south-east corner of the airfield, which had a telephone to ensure quick reaction in an emergency.

Both airships and Sopwiths were restricted by their inability to cope with bad weather but nevertheless a considerable amount of work was done. For example, in July 1917 the airships covered over 5,500 miles on patrol including the escort inwards of three liners loaded with United States troops; the Sopwiths flew nearly 2,500 miles on patrol, from one of which Sub-Lieutenant Allaway failed to return. The airships also suffered casualties; on 13 September 1917 one SS 42A broke away from the hands of its ground party "owing to the pilot, Lieutenant Cripps, for some unexplained reason opening out the engine to full throttle". Both aircraft and crew were lost, wreckage being picked up north of Bull Point.

Also in 1917 a seaplane station was established at Fishguard on "the most convenient site in the neighbourhood" north of the railway station, with a runway to the quay. There was a canvas-and-wood hangar and the Great Western Railway Company provided two carriages on the site until more permanent accommodation was built by the local firm of Topham, Jones and Railton. A 35-foot motor launch was provided by Pembroke Dockyard and the initial complement of aircraft was three single seater Fairey Hamble Babies and three Short 184s of Nos. 426 and 427 Coastal Patrol Flights of No. 245 Squadron.

Both of the air stations came under No. 14 Group Headquarters, which was initially at Pembroke and from July 1917 at Haverfordwest. In addition the group administered a sub-station at Wexford and No.9 Kite Balloon Base at Milford Haven.

The records of both air stations are incomplete, but although the most important contribution of the air patrols was the deterrent effect of their presence on enemy submarines, they were not without action. In October 1917 at least two U boats were attacked from the air, one as it was about to engage two merchant ships. The U boat was forced to break off and submerge but, as was so often the case in attacks on hulls below the surface, the effect of the four bombs which had been dropped could not be assessed. In November 1917 a Fairey seaplane attacked a submarine at periscope depth with four 65lb bombs; in December other similar attacks were reported, one at least of them being thought to have resulted in the sinking of the enemy vessel.

By January 1918 Pembroke was considered to be one of the most important airship stations engaged on anti-submarine work. Operating such vulnerable machines in exposed conditions was no simple matter. In one recorded incident an airship returning from convoy escort found itself flying backwards for over an hour at full throttle in a 40mph headwind. When one of the airship sheds was so seriously damaged by fire that only three inflated machines could be housed, quarries in the area were considered as possible sheltered moorings, one in the neighbourhood of St. Florence being found suitable. February 1918 brought a succession of high winds unprecedented in local memory, and the resulting drop in activity was made worse by the explosion of an SSZ airship with its load of bombs, destroying also the shed in which it had been housed.

Spring weather brought better conditions, and in March 1918 the airships flew over 8,600 patrol miles, including a night operation when a U boat was active in the mouth of the Haven; one submarine was attacked eight miles south-west of Bardsey Island. In April five SSZs and one SS 14A totalled nearly 15,000 patrol miles, enemy submarines being very active. All eight outward convoys from Milford were escorted by two or three airships, and four other convoys were escorted through the area.

May 1918 saw another 15,000 miles of airship patrols, twelve of the sorties being of over eleven hours and fifty of over seven hours. The greatest submarine activity was off the coast of north Cornwall and in the Irish Sea, west of Bardsey. Several attacks were made on submerged submarines, the SSZs now being able to carry two 230lb bombs in place of their previous load of four 100lb ones. However, while armament capable of sinking a submarine was essential, the dependence on human eyesight and their low approach speed made airships ineffective in attack, nevertheless the deterrent effect of their presence was invaluable. In 1918 DH6 training aircraft were introduced into coastal patrolling for just this purpose; though incapable of action they acted as 'scarecrows'. They were based at Pembroke and operated as Nos. 519 and 520 Flights.

The complement of the station at Sageston was about 350 men for the operation of the airships and about 60 for the Sopwiths. There were some 50 members of the women's services, WRNS and later WRAF. Social life for the station was centred on Pembroke and Tenby and their concert parties found time to perform in several places in aid of local charities.

With the arrival of the armistice in 1918, demobilisation and run down was slow and it was March 1920 before the last servicemen left and the station was taken over by the Disposal Board. The remaining buildings were sold by public auction in June 1921.

III - BETWEEN THE WARS

Pembroke Dock
Carew Cheriton

Shipping approaching Great Britain from the west has to pass north or south of Ireland to reach port. The north western approaches could be protected from Scotland and Northern Ireland but the south-western approaches presented a more difficult problem because of the neutrality of Eire, and air cover could only be provided from further back in south-west England and Pembrokeshire. The development of the flying boat and the obvious qualities of the Milford Haven anchorage therefore led to the establishment of Pembroke Dock as a base during the inter-war years.

Preparations there began in 1929 and, although it was not ready for occupation, the station was officially opened on 1 January 1930. When, on

15 June 1931, No. 210 Squadron moved in it found there were as yet no sheds or slipway and its two Southampton flying boats had to be moored out. A third aircraft was soon added but as the Southamptons had previously been based at Basra the first task of the squadron at its new home was to deal with deterioration of its craft due to tropical conditions. There were also problems with the quality of the fresh water supply, but in November the installation of a chlorination plant in the town system persuaded the Air Ministry to cancel plans to evacuate their new base, and work on the necessary facilities continued.

In April/May 1932 a floating dock arrived which greatly improved conditions for working on the aircraft, and in November the station was entrusted with the service trials of the Singapore Mark II boats. In October 1933 it merited a visit from Lord Londonderry, the Secretary of State for Air, and in April 1934 from his Under-Secretary, Sir Philip Sassoon.

On 24 April 1934 the station opened its gates to the public for the first time, entertaining 2,182 visitors. Shortly afterwards, on 20 May, Royal Air Force Pembroke Dock was established with its own headquarters and No. 210 Squadron, which had until then administered the base, became a separate unit, now equipped with Singapore Mark IIIs and under the command of Squadron Leader A.F. Lang, MBE. It took as its badge a griffin segreant, with the motto "Yn y nwyfre yn hedfan" - Hovering in the heavens. This description was put to the test when a Singapore landed on the small lake at Hever Castle (Kent) after two of its tail struts had broken off in flight. Once repaired the boat was roped to a tree and when all four engines were at full throttle the second pilot, on the bank, chopped the rope, reporting that "a very short take off ensued" as he ducked for safety.

The new arrangements provided a basis for expansion and on 1 December 1934 a new squadron of Singapore IIIs, No. 230, was formed at Pembroke Dock, training on 210's aircraft until its own Singapores arrived in the following April.

In January 1935 No. 210 Squadron departed to deliver four Singapore IIIs to No. 205 Squadron in Singapore; only three arrived. The fourth, after experiencing several delays with engine trouble, flew into a mountain near Messina while on passage from Naples to Malta, all the occupants being killed. The remaining crews arrived back in June to be re-equipped with Singapores. In August 1935 four Rangoons of No. 203 Squadron arrived from Basra to be exchanged for Singapore IIIs, No. 210 Squadron taking over the Rangoons. Stranraers, Southamptons and Londons were also to be seen at Pembroke Dock at this time, as the facilities which the base could offer for inspections now included hangar accommodation.

The year 1935 saw the Italian invasion of Abyssinia and in September both the Pembroke Dock squadrons were redeployed to the Mediterranean; No. 210 Squadron went to Gibraltar and No. 230 to Aboukir in Egypt. In their absence the station was reduced to care and maintenance state with a complement of two officers and eighteen other ranks.

In August 1936 the squadrons returned but in October 230 Squadron was off again, this time to Singapore. No. 228 Squadron was formed to replace it. This new squadron was equipped with three Singapores, one Scapa and one London, the mixed bag being due to the delayed delivery of their intended Stranraers.

In April 1937 the squadrons took part in a Mediterranean exercise but were back in time to celebrate the Coronation of King George VI on 12 May with a flight over Swansea, and they also attended the review of the fleet at Spithead on 19th May.

Exercises in coastal and trade defence, anti-submarine tactics, co-operation with the Home Fleet and night flying practice occupied the time. A side effect of the Spanish Civil War was submarine activity against merchant shipping in the western Mediterranean, British and French maritime aircraft being deployed for protection. This included a three-month detachment of 210 Squadron to Arzeu in Algeria from September 1937.

Training was not without its hazards and in March 1938 one of No. 228 Squadron's Stranraers crashed off Brest with the loss of all five of its crew. In September 1938 a Sunderland, making a night landing in Angle Bay, turned over and broke its back, two of its eight crew being killed.

Sunderland aircraft were soon to be the backbone of Coastal Command in war, training and conversion being concentrated at Pembroke Dock. Nos. 210 and 230 Squadrons were the first. In June 1938 a Sunderland on a delivery flight to Singapore set a new record of eight hours for the leg to Gibraltar. In August five aircraft en route to a Mediterranean exercise had to return from Lisbon owing to difficulties with newly-modified airscrews but the crews had the pleasure of having their problems there dealt with by the British Air Attache with the distinctive name of Wing Commander P.R.T.J.M.I.C. Chamberlayne.

The Munich crisis in September 1938 caused the recall of all Pembroke Dock personnel from leave and the departure of the squadrons to their war stations; No. 210 Squadron went to Tayport (Fife) and No. 228 to Invergordon (Ross and Cromarty), to where the floating dock also set off at the end of a tow rope. On the resumption of normal relations with Germany in October all returned to Pembroke Dock and settled down once more. In November the Old Dockyard Church was reopened for use by all denominations.

The most notable feature of the flying boat squadrons at this time was flexibility. In March 1939 No. 240 Squadron was based at Calshot (Southampton Water) but carried out an operational exercise from Pembroke Dock; in June No. 228 Squadron, now also equipped with Sunderlands, left for Alexandria to join Middle East Command. On 15 June Pembroke Dock was put under the command of No. 15 Group.

The capability of Pembroke Dock was reinforced by the reopening of Carew Cheriton - R.N. Air Station Pembroke of twenty years before - early in the year. By June 1939 it housed seven Ansons of C Flight, 217 Squadron, whose main base was Tangmere (Sussex). However, with a bomb load of four 100lb weapons and no detection equipment the Anson was hardly an improvement on the aircraft which had operated from there in 1918. An Anti-Aircraft Cooperation Flight of Henleys was also based at Carew.

On the outbreak of war Carew Cheriton was brought into No. 15 Group and No. 217 Squadron transferred from Fighter Command to Coastal Command, the squadron headquarters moving to St. Eval (Cornwall). Pembroke Dock became responsible for the administration of the station.

Pembroke Dock, now commanded by Group Captain Twistleton-Wykeham-Fiennes, had only No. 210 Squadron equipped with six Sunderlands at readiness, four more on detachment at Woodhaven, two more front line aircraft in immediate reserve and three more in store. There was also one Sunderland of No. 228 Squadron. No. 210 confidently reported that it was "up to scratch and everything under control" and, in the event, in the early morning of 3 September one of its Sunderlands, captained by Flight Lieutenant Ainslie, was on patrol with seven destroyers on the convoy route to Milford Haven. Coastal Command had been mobilised during August for a large scale operational exercise and this was still in progress.

The first report of the war was "No merchant vessels present; no enemy sighted". One Anson of 217 Squadron was also in the air on anti-submarine patrol at 11.15 am; it was recalled to base to be bombed up.

Also at Pembroke Dock were eight officers and fourteen airmen of the Royal Australian Air Force. The RAAF had purchased nine Sunderlands earlier in the year and these men were being trained on the type by No. 210 Squadron and were waiting for delivery of their machines.

With the squadrons at readiness and the defence of the vulnerable points in the good hands of one officer and twenty-eight other ranks of the 15th Welch Regiment, Royal Air Force stations Pembroke Dock and Carew Cheriton went to war.

* * *

IV - WAR OPERATIONS

1. The Opening Shots   Pembroke Dock
                                                                                                          Carew Cheriton

    The operational task of No. 217 Squadron's Ansons was to escort convoys of merchant ships in the Bristol Channel, St. George's Channel and Carmarthen Bay and to carry out specific searches for submarines and mines. The flying boats were now able to range further and the first few days saw them patrolling as far as Norway.

    Reinforcements soon arrived. As Italy was showing signs of remaining neutral, No. 228 Squadron returned from the Mediterranean on 10 September, one aircraft crashing on landing in very poor weather. On 16 September six Ansons of No. 206 Squadron joined Carew Cheriton. The first attack on an enemy submarine was on 9 September by a Sunderland of 210 Squadron; as so often in air attacks on submerging or submerged U boats, the only evidence of possible damage was a patch of oil on the surface.

    Carew Cheriton also started the war well when on 20 September two Ansons, flown by Pilot Officer Patrick and Sergeant Hughes, attacked a submarine eight miles west of Lundy and claimed it as a 'probable'.

    Sunderland L 2165, Pembroke Dock's first aircraft to attack a submarine, was also its first war casualty, crashing off Dale on 17 September when returning from a patrol.

    The early days of the war were very active, probably because of the initial deployment of the enemy submarine force. On 11 September No. 210 Squadron aircraft searched for a submarine which had sunk a British merchant ship 200 miles to the north-west of Ireland; the submarine was not found, but an American ship was led to the rescue of two boat loads of survivors. On 14 September Sunderland L 2167 of No. 210 Squadron attacked a submarine which had torpedoed the SS Vancouver City, remaining with the two lifeboats until the occupants were picked up by the Dutch vessel Moravia.

    On 16 and 17 September No. 210 Squadron attacked two more submarines, one attack with apparent success. On 18 September Sunderland N 9025 picked up a message from the SS Kensington Court that it had been torpedoed and was sinking; a heavily loaded lifeboat was seen with 34 survivors. The flying boat landed and took off the captain and nineteen others; the rest were rescued similarly by a second Sunderland. L 2167 found and attacked a submarine in the area but with uncertain result. On 19 September No. 210 Squadron attacked another U boat and on 24th N 9023 reported a direct hit on a submarine which had attacked the SS Hazelside, before briefing a fishing vessel to pick up the survivors.

At Carew Cheriton the action on 20 September was the only engagement of the opening month of the war. This was not surprising in that the task of convoy escort was designed to protect shipping by the aircraft's presence and the effectiveness of a patrol was measured at best by the non-event. In poor weather, and without the aids to navigation which were developed later in the war, escort was a difficult and somewhat chancy business. Failure of the aircraft to locate their charges did not always lie at their door; sometimes the reported positions of the convoys themselves were inaccurate, and aircraft arriving at a stated rendezvous in poor visibility to find nothing might well fail to pick up the ships within their radius of search.

Because Coastal Command had too few aircraft to meet all demands, 'Scarecrow patrols' as flown by the DH 6s of 1918 were introduced once more and No. 5 Coastal Flight of Tiger Moths joined the Ansons at Carew. They were unarmed but they helped to provide air cover in inshore waters.

The embryo No. 10 Squadron, Royal Australian Air Force was put at the disposal of the RAF by the Australian government and bases in Australia were combed for volunteers to make up its numbers while the pilots already at Pembroke Dock continued their training by flying on patrol with Nos. 210 and 228 Squadrons. By the end of September No. 10 Squadron started equipping with its own aircraft and Coastal Command took over responsibility for its administration.

The end of the first month of the war saw a change of command for Pembroke Dock when Group Captain R.J. Bone, CB, CBE, DSO took over on 24 September.

2. To the End of 1940

Pembroke Dock
Carew Cheriton

After the early engagements resulting from the initial dispositions of both submarines and surface shipping, the air/sea war settled down to a long campaign of changing fortunes, following the geographical pattern of the war in Europe and the technological development of both submarines and search aircraft.

Escorts and patrols from Carew were mainly uneventful, which fact could be expected in view of the station's inshore operating area and the limited capability of its aircraft. In November 1939 one of the Tiger Moths came down in the sea one mile north-east of Caldey, a search by the Tenby Lifeboat and an RAF launch failing to find the pilot's body. The Tiger Moth flight was disbanded in May 1940, by which time the development of German tactics had made the scarecrow patrols ineffective.

On 7 February 1940 an Anson took part in a search for the SS Eldon Park but found the Tenby Lifeboat on the spot with the situation in hand. On

25 February another Anson was sent off to attack a U boat which had been reported off Caldey, but the crew decided that the destroyer and two armed trawlers which were in the area were better equipped for the task; the eyeball was the Ansons' only search device and there was no way by which they could detect a submerged submarine. Their main role was to deter the enemy from coming up into an attacking position within torpedo range of the surface ships.

The experience of the flying boats was similar, though their greater range and lookout capabilities produced more sightings. In October 1939 there were several reports of U boat activity within their operational area but the only sighting to provide an opportunity for attack was on 21 October when Sunderland L 5806 of No. 228 Squadron claimed a direct hit on a U boat off south-west Ireland. The other highlight of the month was the arrival of the first contingent of seventeen WAAF at Pembroke Dock under the command of Company Assistant Joyce Neale. They were to be joined by others and to become a fully integrated and indispensable part of the station as they gradually overcame the male reserve which had greeted them.

November 1939 offered even less in the way of surfaced targets unless one can count a Coastguard report of a submarine three miles west of Llansantffraid church (Cardigan Bay) which turned out to be a porpoise.

In December one attack only was reported. On the 8th, Sunderland L 5805 of No. 228 Squadron sighted the conning tower of a diving submarine in the vicinity of the torpedoed SS Brandon and dropped eight 250lb bombs on the spot, without being able to claim any direct hits, although two large oil patches were seen. Two destroyers were guided to the area to carry on the search.

December 1939 also saw the arrival of more Australians to build up No. 10 Squadron, and the airmen of Station Headquarters had to move into the basement of the National School to make room for them in barracks. The new arrivals were visited in January 1940 by the High Commissioner for Australia and the Secretary of State for the Dominions, The Rt. Hon. Anthony Eden, the day being rounded off with an ENSA concert sponsored by Sir Seymour Hicks.

The operational high spot in January was when Sunderland N 9025 of No. 228 Squadron sighted a U boat actually on the surface, with about ten sailors out on deck. As cloud was down to surface level they presumably felt comparatively safe. In spite of cloud difficulties the Sunderland was able to drop one bomb and engage in a gun battle with the boat, which appeared to have been disabled so that it could not submerge. HMS Fowey was left to deal with it and to pick up the eleven survivors.

In February 1940 No. 10 Squadron RAAF became operational, the beginning of the great contribution which that force was to make to the war in

Europe, both with its own squadrons and also by injections of large numbers of individual aircrew into the squadrons of the RAF. The wider pattern of life with the flying boats was demonstrated by Flight Lieutenant Craven of No. 228 Squadron when, en route from Invergordon via Stranraer (Wigtownshire), he delivered 500lb of yeast to Belfast, where all bakeries had run out because of interruption of supplies by sea. He was demonstrating his grasp of flexibility as a principle of war. As Air Marshal Sir Robert Craven, he was to round off his career as Commander Maritime Air Forces.

Such detachments between bases were necessary in order to use the available flying boats to the best effect. March 1940 saw the Pembroke Dock boats escorting army co-operation and fighter aircraft to Norway after the German invasion, and providing navigational guidance, rescue service and transport for the ground crews.

On 1 April No. 10 Squadron left for Mount Batten (Plymouth) and in the next few months there were a number of other changes in the Pembroke Dock establishment. In the meantime Nos. 210 and 228 Squadrons continued to patrol the seas south of Ireland, assisted by craft from Mount Batten and the French Latecoere 523s from Lanevoc. A visitor on 15 April was the Aeronavale flying boat Antares, an aircraft which never gave up, its efforts being at last crowned with success when it sank a U boat in June 1943.

The Norwegian campaign continued to provide variety and, for the flying boats, unusual activities. On 15 April a party under Major General Carton de Wiart was landed in a fjord to rendezvous with a destroyer. While the Sunderland of No. 228 Squadron was on the water transferring its passengers, it was attacked by guns and bombs from four Junkers 88s and two Heinkel 111s but nevertheless managed to take off and return to Invergordon.

On 25th April another Sunderland, captained by Flight Lieutenant Craven, set out from Invergordon to ferry passengers to Norway. At Alesund, near the intended landing, enemy aircraft were seen to be busy bombing the wireless telegraphy station, so the Sunderland went on to Molde Fjord, only to be attacked with bombs by three Junkers 88s. After stopping it was attacked by twelve more. The passengers were disembarked, the captain accompanying them to see if there was a safer anchorage. This was not wholly a good move, as the whaler which was being used as a ferry was hit, and the second pilot was having to take avoiding action by taxying around; his engines overheated and he was forced to take off, leaving his captain behind. A Messerschmitt 110 now attacked the Sunderland, which proceeded to shoot it down before landing again, this time at the original destination.

May 1940 saw the occupation of western France by the Germans, which changed the whole pattern of the anti-submarine war in the south-western approaches. The immediate effect was the loss of the assistance of the French flying boats from Brest, and the Bay of Biscay and the channel approaches were brought within the range of enemy fighter cover. The Germans lost no time in consolidating their position and by 6 July Lorient was ready to receive U boats, bringing their base much closer to the convoy routes and increasing their operating range by avoiding the long trip to the German ports around the north of Scotland. Shipping losses rose immediately to an average of some quarter of a million tons a month.

On 27 May 1940 No. 240 Squadron came down from Invergordon to Pembroke Dock with five London flying boats, in order to convert to Stranraers; it was to leave again on 30 July having contributed to patrol operations during its stay. At the beginning of June 1940 eight Fokker T VIII W twin-engined float planes of the Royal Netherlands Naval Air Service arrived and became No. 320 Squadron. In June No. 321 Squadron was formed out of Dutch personnel to be equipped with Ansons and based at Carew Cheriton. The Fokkers took part in maritime patrols but after three months they ran out of spares and the crews moved to Carew to merge with those already there and to convert on to Hudson aircraft.

On 10 June No. 228 Squadron, having done so much good work, left Pembroke Dock for Malta because of Italy's entry into the war, and on 13 July 210 Squadron went to Oban (Argyllshire). There were more changes during July. No. 764 Squadron, Fleet Air Arm, arrived on 3rd; it was a floatplane training unit equipped with Walrus and Swordfish aircraft, its former base at Lee on Solent having become uncomfortably close to the air front line. The squadron was at Pembroke Dock for nearly a year before moving out to its own base at Lawrenny Ferry, where it remained until it was disbanded in October 1943. The slipway is the only surviving sign of its stay.

Also in July, C Flight of No. 217 Squadron left Carew Cheriton to return to its parent unit at St. Eval. It was replaced, but only until the end of August, by B Flight of No. 48 Squadron with six more Ansons.

No. 209 Squadron moved from Oban to Pembroke Dock in the same month, flying Lerwick aircraft. It was now the only operational squadron there, but was of limited capability as the machines were to be fitted with Hercules II engines and the delivery of these was held up by bomb damage to the Bristol Aircraft factory at Filton. It carried out a little operational flying from Pembroke Dock before it moved on to Stranraer in December.

The operational status of Pembroke Dock was for some time reduced to its use by aircraft from elsewhere as a forward base. This might have had something to do with the enemy air attacks in the area, which started on 15 July when four bombs were dropped near the oil tanks and four more, which did not explode, fell a mile and a half north of Carew Cheriton. On 19 July the airfield was bombed with more effect, three of eleven bombs being within the boundary and close to the runway, but damage and casualties were slight. There was scattered bombing of Pembroke Dock a few days later but with no effect on the air base.

One unexpected result of this enemy air activity was that the No. 48 Squadron detachment at Carew Cheriton, which was engaged in training Dutch crews for escort work, was considered for night fighter operations to counter German mine-laying aircraft, which were at the time regular visitors to the Haven. However, this new and unlikely role for the Ansons did not eventuate, and they left for Islay (Inner Hebrides) on 30 August.

Although operational activity was now very low, ceremonial was at a high level judging by the visits in July and August 1940 of Marshal of the RAF Lord Trenchard, Group Captain HRH The Duke of Kent, and Prince Bernhardt of the Netherlands.

The rest of 1940 was marked by more enemy air raids, but little damage to the Pembroke Dock base resulted. Carew Cheriton did not fare so well, and in October a hangar was destroyed by a raid, with serious damage to another hangar in addition to other buildings. Two Ansons and a Henley were burned out.

A minor but interesting feature of the Royal Air Force extablishment in Pembrokeshire in this autumn of 1940 was No. 21 Balloon Centre Pembroke Dock; No. 962 Squadron had twenty-four kite balloons deployed north and south of the Haven, which covered all the vital points. The personnel were accommodated in Corston House, Pembroke and Magnet House and the Atlantic Hotel, Milford Haven. The balloons provided useful deterrence to low-flying aircraft but were not without risk to our own forces. On 12 October a Sunderland ran into a cable and damaged its wing, at the same time releasing the balloon and 2,000ft of trailing wire. On 2 November a gale set eighteen balloons adrift with or without their cables. No. 962 Squadron moved to Pembrey in December, unmourned by the flying boat crews.

The end of the year found Pembroke Dock without a resident operational squadron, and No. 320 Netherlands Squadron at Carew Cheriton just completing its conversion training on to Hudsons. An important new organisation, the Coastal Command Development Unit, was formed at Carew in December; it overstretched the local accommodation, consequently the officers had to move into the Royal Gate House Hotel, Tenby and the airman into Ashleigh House, Sageston.

3. 1941   Pembroke Dock
                                                                        Carew Cheriton

The movements of the previous year meant that Pembroke Dock started 1941 with only detached flying boats from other stations, while No. 320 Netherlands Squadron, now converted to Hudsons, was at Carew Cheriton. The facilities at Pembroke Dock were used for the maintenance of aircraft from elsewhere; for example No. 201 Squadron, covering the northern approaches from Scottish (including Shetland) bases, sent its boats down for major servicing. Some of the aircraft detached to Pembroke Dock were prepared for overseas service and formed into a new unit, No. 95 Squadron, which moved off to Freetown in Sierra Leone.

On 30 January 1941 a Catalina arrived from Bermuda bound for Greenock; this was the beginning of a flow of these aircraft, which had a greater operational range than the Sunderland and provided Coastal Command with valuable reinforcement.

In March 1941 there was a change at Carew Cheriton when the Dutch squadron left for Leuchars (Fife). It was replaced by the Blenheims of No. 236 Squadron from St. Eval. Their role was still convoy escort; as well being able to carry bombs they were more capable than their predecessors at Carew of providing protection from the enemy aircraft which were increasingly to be found in their operating area. On the squadron's first day at Carew flying Officer Innis and his crew drove off two He 111s which were attacking four merchant vessels south of Caldey Island. On 15 April three aircraft were scrambled to intercept four Ju 88s off Fastnet rock. One of the enemy aircraft was damaged before the Blenheims had to break off through lack of fuel and ammunition. Their limitations were shown up in their inferior performance to that of the Ju 88s but the enemy treated them with respect. Also on 15 April four of the Blenheims were damaged during a raid on Carew Cheriton in which 20 to 25 high explosive bombs and 100 incendiary bombs were dropped.

Although there had been numerous enemy raids in the area the first damage to the flying boat base was in the early hours of 12 May when about twenty enemy aircraft dropped at least twelve 500Kg land mines, one of which caused material damage. The clothing and barrack stores, the operations block and the armoury were all destroyed and the officers' mess severely damaged. One man was killed. The WAAF hostel was damaged but nevertheless the airwomen combined dealing with incendiaries with providing tea and moral support for civilians caught out in the raid. On 14 May an RAF high-speed launch was destroyed at the entrance to the Haven.

Brest, Lorient, St. Nazaire, La Pallice and Bordeaux were now all enemy submarine bases. Their main operating area had become the mid-Atlantic where the convoys were out of range of escorting aircraft from either shore. The coastal squadrons therefore put their main effort into patrolling the concentration areas through which the U boats had to pass: the Scotland/Iceland gap and the Bay of Biscay. The latter was divided up into search areas which fanned out from the Scillies towards the north-east of Spain. The Pembroke Dock aircraft helped to patrol these. Although some three-quarters of the Coastal Command aircraft were by now fitted with ASV Mk II radar it was as yet of limited effectiveness, and most sightings were still by eye.

In March 1941 the German 'pocket battleships' Scharnhorst and Gneisnau took refuge in Brest on their return from commerce raiding in the Atlantic, and a constant watch had to be kept for their possible breakout. Aircraft patrolling the Bay now had frequent brushes with the enemy fighters which had been brought down to French airfields.

No. 10 Squadron RAAF, based at Mount Batten, operated occasional aircraft from Pembroke Dock during this time, and their sorties from the Haven were not without incident. One of its Sunderlands was involved in a fight with a Heinkel 115 on 18 April; the next day another located a ship's lifeboat with 37 men on board. On 19 April one of its aircraft lost its way in St. George's Channel, for a time wandering over the Irish Republic. The crew refused to jump and face internment, and an attempt was made to land in the sea near Bardsey Island. The aircraft sank, five of the crew being saved.

At the end of May 1941 No. 10 Squadron returned to Pembroke Dock. On 5 June one of its aircraft was attacked by two Arado 196 seaplane fighters, of which one was shot down and the other driven off; on 30 June there was another air battle with two Focke Wolf 200s, the long-range commerce raider and U boat co-operation aircraft. One No. 10 Squadron Sunderland on 9 July landed on the open sea to pick up four survivors of submarine attack from their dinghy, but in doing so it suffered damage which made take off impossible. The crew set out to taxi back to England on only three engines but they were picked up on the way by a Royal Navy destroyer which then sank the aircraft by gunfire. At this time the squadron was equipped with six Sunderlands and one Catalina, and since its formation had flown nearly 9,000 hours on patrol.

In August 1941, No. 119 Squadron arrived at Pembroke Dock, but its short stay added little to the station's operational effectiveness. The squadron had been formed in September 1940 to operate three large Short S 26 Grenadier Class flying boats, named Golden Fleece, Golden Hind and Golden Horn, which had been built before the war for the Atlantic passenger route. On the outbreak of war they were converted with three four-gun Boulton Paul turrets and eight bomb racks for military use. However, by the time the squadron arrived at Pembroke Dock it was equipped with Catalinas, and spent the next two months converting to Sunderlands, leaving in December.

Aircraft of other squadrons appear in Pembroke Dock patrol reports during the latter part of the year; the Sunderlands of No. 228 Squadron had arrived back from the Middle East during August, but only to wait for the arrival of their ground crews before going on to Invergordon in October. No. 209 Squadron returned from Iceland in October, having exchanged its

Lerwicks for Catalinas. Individual aircraft of No. 210 Squadron also appear in records for the latter part of 1941.

No. 10 Squadron was however the residential operational unit and was fully engaged. It recorded U boat attacks on 10 and 30 September and also on 7 October, but with doubtful result in each case. On 22 October one of its Sunderlands made a successful landing at sea to rescue the survivors of a crashed Whitley.

A Catalina of No. 209 Squadron attacked a submarine on 30 October but again with uncertain success. One of that squadron's aircraft crashed on 14 December, nine of its crew of eleven being killed. On 23 December a Catalina of No. 240 Squadron sank after attempting a night landing in Angle Bay.

The need for higher performance to deal with Ju 88s was recognised in October 1941 by the addition of three Beaufighters to the strength of No. 236 Squadron at Carew Cheriton. As well as their normal escort duties, both the Blenheims and the Beaufighters went on intruder sorties and reconnaissance flights in the Brest peninsula, attacking land targets and checking on the German warships in harbour, using St. Eval as a forward base. One of their routine tasks was to escort the Fishguard - Rosslare ferry and the civil DC3 flights from Ireland to Chivenor in Devon. In October 1941 an aircraft on this duty was forced to land in Ireland, resulting in the crew members being interned.

The year 1941 ended with the departure of No. 10 Squadron from Pembroke Dock, leaving No. 209 Squadron with its Catalinas as the only resident unit. However, both it and No. 236 Squadron at Carew were soon to be caught up in the constant round of redeployments.

4. 1942

Pembroke Dock
Carew Cheriton
Talbenny
Dale

1942 opened at Carew Cheriton with a visit on 6 January by Prince Peter of Greece accompanied by General Sikorski, though neither Greek nor Polish forces were stationed there. Operationally, No. 238 Squadron went over entirely to Beaufighter aircraft. The crews which were already proficient with this type of aircraft carried on with convoy escort and reconnaissance over Brest until they were taken off operations on 20 January. Conversion training continued, there being three crashes in the process, and the squadron left en route for the Middle East on 8 February.

The role of Carew Cheriton as an operational station was coming to an end. On 11 February 1942 No. 254 Squadron, equipped with Blenheims, moved in from Dyce (Aberdeen) to continue escort duties but stayed only until June. On three occasions in March they drove enemy aircraft away from their charges. They lost one of their machines to anti-aircraft fire off Ushant, and another in an accident in Carmarthen Bay; the crew of this aircraft were picked up by the Tenby Lifeboat but did not survive.

The departure of No. 254 Squadron marked the end of operations from Carew Cheriton, apart from a few Hurricanes of Nos. 32 and 238 Squadrons on detachment from Pembrey. On 24 July 1942 the station was transferred from No. 19 Group, Coastal Command to No. 25 Group, Flying Training Command.

At Pembroke Dock 209 Squadron's Catalinas carried on with their duties until they were transferred overseas at the end of March 1942. From then until September there were no resident squadrons at Pembroke Dock, but aircraft operating there from time to time included Catalinas of Nos. 209, 210, 240 and 413 Squadrons and Sunderlands of 461, mainly engaged on Bay of Biscay patrols and checking shipping, including French and Spanish fishing boats, making occasional attacks on German U boats and having brushes with enemy aircraft.

On 6 September No. 119 Squadron returned with its Sunderlands, and on 4 October 210 Squadron with Catalinas from the Shetlands, to give the station its own squadrons once more.

Although Carew Cheriton had ceased to be operational and Pembroke Dock was for much of 1942 operating at a low rate, more interesting things were taking place nearby. On 1 May Talbenny opened as a station in No. 19 Group with Dale as its satellite. They were both bleak and exposed cliff-top sites where flying conditions could be difficult and the servicing of aircraft in winter a gruelling business, but they became the homes of some very hard men, of No. 304 (Polish) Squadron and No. 311 (Czech) Squadron, transferred from Bomber Command to strengthen the anti-submarine coverage.

Such reductions in the bomber force were very much against the will of its Commander-in-Chief, who was convinced that submarines could best be countered by his force attacking their concentration points, their home ports, the shipyards in which they were built and repaired and the factories which supplied them. Certainly a great contribution to the submarine war was being made in this way, but it was a matter of balance and someone had to deal with those U boats which got away to sea.

No. 304 (Polish) Squadron had been formed in the Royal Air Force in June 1940 out of Polish airmen who had been serving in the French forces before being evacuated to Britain. No. 311 (Czech) Squadron, equipped with Wellington Mk. ICs, arrived at Talbenny on 12 June 1942; on 15th June No. 304 Squadron also flying Wellingtons moved into Dale. Before either squadron had operated from its new home, seven crews from 304 and fourteen from 311 were detached to Bircham Newton (Norfolk), to join their old Command in the '1000 bomber' Bremen raid on 25 June. One of the No. 304 Squadron aircraft was lost in the operation; one from No. 311 crashed on return.

By the end of June 1942 the squadrons were carrying out anti-submarine patrols in the approaches to St. George's Channel and down into the Bay of Biscay. In July, 311 attacked two submarines, both being damaged and one of them probably sunk. No. 304 Squadron attacked four with encouraging results, one of them a very large boat, believed to be Italian. They also met enemy aircraft and acquitted themselves well, shooting down an Arado 196 seaplane in one of the encounters. An aircraft of No. 311 Squadron was lost during the month. Both squadrons earned the congratulations of the Air Officer Commander in Chief of Coastal Command on their good start in their new role.

August was an excellent month for the Czechs, who flew 104 sorties and made seven attacks on U boats, of which most were thought to be unlikely to make port. No. 304 Squadron made two submarine attacks, sinking one and damaging another. In addition to going on patrol the Wellingtons attacked the submarine base at La Pallice, near La Rochelle. On this raid, No. 311 Squadron lost an aircraft, probably to enemy fighters. No.304 Squadron lost one aircraft in an accident off Anglesey and a second while attempting the first operational night take off from Dale, the crew of six being drowned.

General Sikorski awarded No. 304 (Polish) Squadron the title of No. 304 Polish Bomber Squadron of the County of Slask. The spirit of the Polish forces in exile was exemplified by the Commanding Officer, Wing Commander Poziomek, on handing over to his successor:

> "The asset which we must bring Poland is not the number of flights made or aircraft serviced but the knowledge, experience and unity gained. Poland has many times held the keys to greatness but has lost them because of human selfishness and unbounded individualism. We must realise a firm conviction. There shall be no forgiveness to the selfishness of one man - our aim must be the good of Poland."

September 1942 was a very active month for the Wellingtons. During 101 sorties No. 311 Squadron made three attacks and in each case the submarine was damaged. One of the three submarines demonstrated a new tactic, of which more would be seen, by fighting it out with the aircraft without submerging, and with such effect that the Wellington had to crash land at St. Eval when returning, with five of the crew injured. A 304 Squadron aircraft had a gun battle with a submarine off the north coast of Spain, before damaging it to the extent that it had to seek sanctuary in a neutral port. The squadron also attacked a tanker at sea and shipping in Bordeaux harbour.

There were numerous encounters with enemy aircraft in which the Wellingtons gave a good account of themselves. In one, Wellington HF 836 of 304 Squadron fought a notable battle with six Ju 88s; one of the German aircraft was shot down and another made off with large pieces breaking off its tail plane; all the rest were damaged. The Wellington managed to get back to land at Portreath (Cornwall) in spite of being holed in many places. Another Ju 88 was shot down before the end of the month. The Junkers 88 was a formidable aircraft, armed with three 20mm cannon and three machine guns, and the odds were very much in its favour.

The increasing enemy air opposition brought Beaufighters of Nos. 235 and 248 Squadrons to Talbenny for four months from mid-September 1942. During their stay they intercepted Ju 88s on several occasions, shooting down three. They also had their losses, two out of a patrol of three being shot down by FW 190s in December. Another mysteriously went missing near base.

Anti-submarine operations in the last quarter of the year were affected by the weather and by the concentration of enemy boats off North Africa which followed the Torch landings. In October 1942 each squadron reported one attack, and then there were no more for the rest of the year. In November No. 304 Squadron, which spent the month at Talbenny while work was in progress at Dale, attacked an enemy convoy of four merchant ships.

There were casualties. No. 304 Squadron lost two Wellingtons on operations and one in an accident in St. Bride's Bay; an aircraft of 311 crashed with the loss of all crew and passengers while it was on a communication flight to Coastal Command headquarters. Among the successes, one 311 Squadron Wellington survived an attack by seven JU 88s and one Fiat BR 20, damaging two of the Junkers; another shot down one Ju 88 and damaged two others out of four attackers.

On 29 December 1942 a No. 311 Squadron aircraft found a tanker south of Ireland flying no flag and with no crew to be seen. It proved to be the British ship Regent Lion which had been abandoned in the Atlantic four months earlier but had survived to return home without a crew; it was recovered.

5. Fighter Defence
Angle

The provision of Coastal Command Beaufighters at Carew Cheriton and Talbenny was rather spasmodic and they were used, in part, on longer range sorties towards the French coast, but short range fighter cover was not neglected, at least between mid-1941 and early 1943.

Royal Air Force, Angle was opened in June 1941 in No. 10 Group, Fighter Command as part of the Fairwood Common (Glamorgan) sector. The first aircraft to operate from the windswept cliff overlooking Freshwater West were the Hurricanes of No. 32 Squadron from Pembrey (Carmarthenshire).

Short 184 floatplane, which operated from Fishguard Harbour 1917-18

Sopwith 1700 "1½ Strutter" based at RNAS Pembroke 1917-18

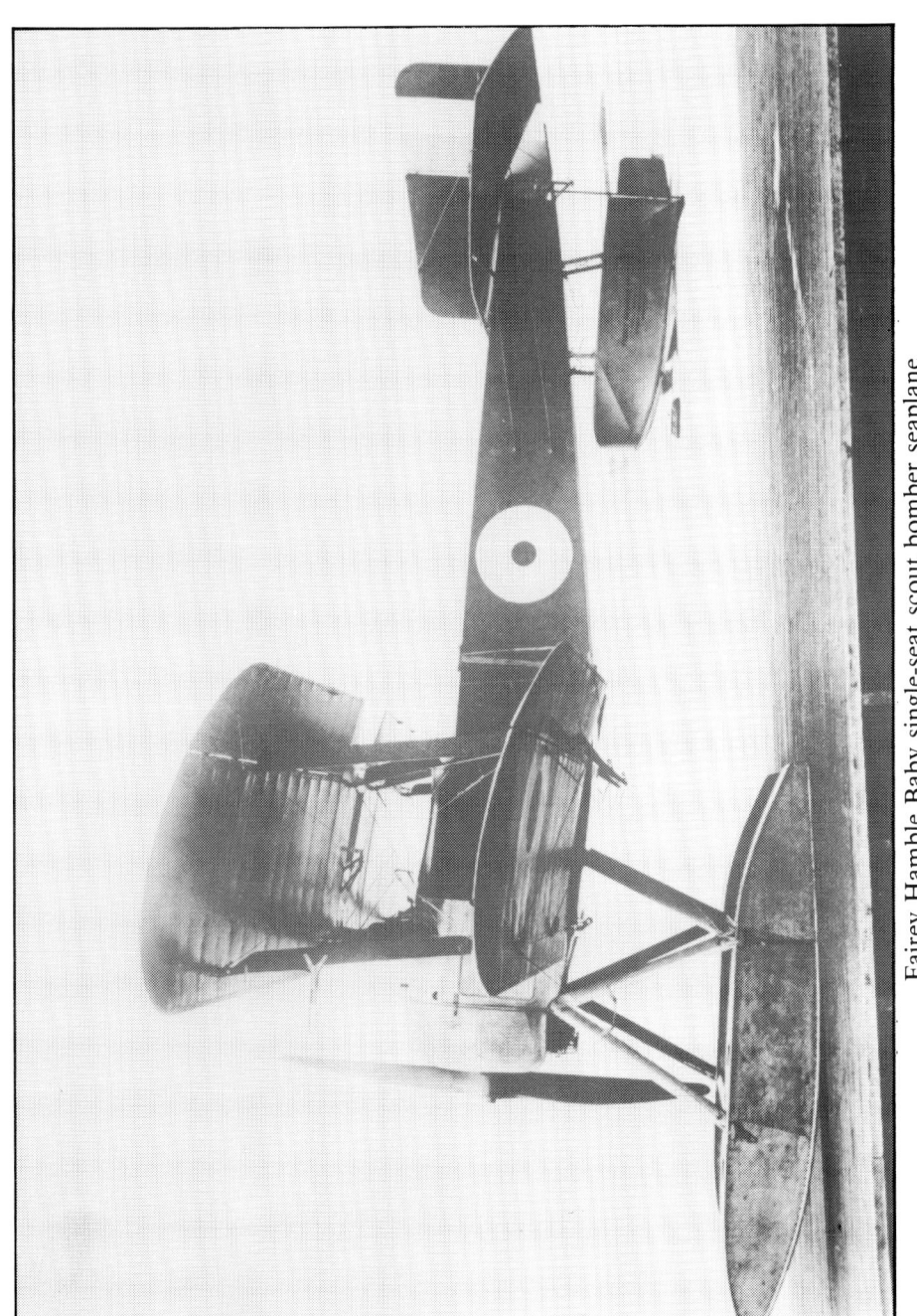

Fairey Hamble Baby single-seat scout bomber seaplane

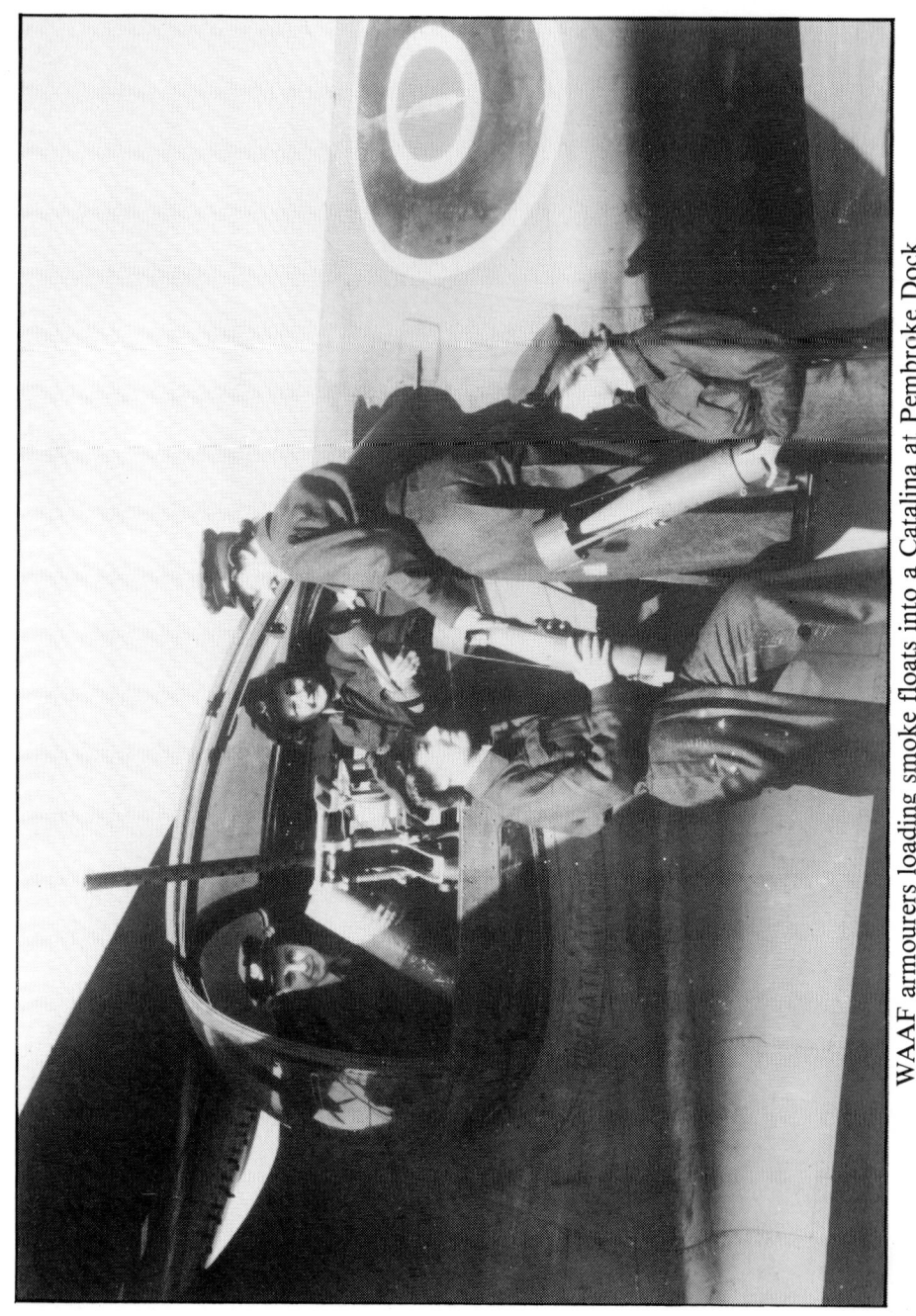

WAAF armourers loading smoke floats into a Catalina at Pembroke Dock

Avro Anson I of 217 Squadron, over Giltar

Short Sunderland of 10 Squadron RAAF

Wellington Ic's of 311 Squadron

Westland Whirlwind of 263 Squadron

Their role was to protect close-in convoys from air attack, a task which had stretched the capabilities of the Blenheims of No. 236 Squadron at Carew. They promptly set to and on 4 June probably destroyed a Dornier bomber as well as damaging a Heinkel 111. On 10 June a Ju 88 was shot down, though the pilot of one of the two Hurricanes engaging it had to land his craft in Eire. The squadron was kept busy, flying up to thirty sorties a day until November 1941 when it moved to Manston (Kent). Its losses included two aircraft missing on patrol, and one which crashed at Freshwater East on return from an operational sortie, the pilot being killed.

No. 32 Squadron was replaced on 27 November by No. 615 (County of Surrey) Squadron, Royal Auxiliary Air Force, equipped with long range Hurricane IIBs. The desolation of the Angle site was an unwelcome change from Manston and their record book opened with the comment that "the first sight of our new station confirms our worst fears - but we shall get used to it in time." They quickly settled down to operations, badly damaging a Ju 88 three days after their arrival and in December providing air cover for day bombing attacks on Brest, using Perranporth (Cornwall) for forward refuelling. Also in December, off the Smalls, they located a British destroyer which had been damaged by enemy aircraft and guided in the rescue ships which towed the destroyer into Milford.

Christmas Day was not the gayest in the squadron's experience, notwithstanding a greetings telegram from their Honorary Air Commodore, the Prime Minister, then in the United States. However, Pembroke Dock offered some welcome hospitality and the sea air, which as they observed was "all that Angle provides" proved an effective cure for sore heads.

On 11 January 1942 the record book notes that "Flight Lieutenant Dunsford gave us a very interesting lecture on escaping technique but was unable to give us any hints on how to escape from Angle". Rescue was at hand in the form of a move to Fairwood Common before the end of the month. They were replaced from there by No. 312 (Czech) Squadron with Spitfires. The arrival of the the Czechs at Angle was not auspicious; while undertaking an operational patrol en route, one aircraft made a forced landing at Trevine (North Pembrokeshire) and the pilot of another had to bale out near Aberystwyth.

The Angle airfield was still only partially completed, and the officers in particular were housed in very primitive conditions. The winter weather brought very rapid changes of visibility, and strong gales damaged both servicing hangars. The earth banks, which were put up to give some shelter to aircraft and servicing crews, are still to be seen on the cliff top and will no doubt interest the archaeologists of the future. Inspections of any length had to be carried out at Fairwood Common and Carew Cheriton. In spite of the conditions at Angle, the squadron had its successes. On 16 February Pilot Officer Kucrea shot down a Ju 88; another Junkers was probably destroyed on 21 March, the Spitfire pilot getting back in spite of being shot in the thigh. On 18 April 1942 the squadron returned to Fairwood Common; at this time Angle was a station to be taken in small doses.

Its replacement, No. 263 Squadron, was one of the only two squadrons in the RAF to be equipped with the Westland Whirlwind, a twin engined fighter and the first in the service to be fitted with cannon - four 20mm Hispanos in the nose. It was a faster aircraft at low level than the contemporary Spitfire but it had handling problems which contributed to decisions about its further development.

If No. 312 Squadron had had an eventful journey to Angle, 263's was more dramatic. When the train carrying the ground crews and equipment was passing through Llanelli, the wooden truck next to the engine and containing A Flight's armoury was found to be on fire. It was hurried into a siding where the Llanelli fire brigade was able to douse it before the ammunition exploded, but not before being treated to a brilliant display of Verey lights.

No. 263 Squadron did well at Angle, helped no doubt by the end of winter. They flew what was for them a record 818 hours in May, including the longest operational flight so far by a Whirlwind when two of them chased an enemy aircraft as far as Dublin. Their hours also added up to one of the highest accident-free totals recorded in Fighter Command at this time. They made one or two attacks with their cannon on German airfields in France, with Spitfires as escorts, but their use from Angle in this role was limited by the necessity to transport their specialised ground crews to a forward base for arming and servicing.

Life at Angle was now settling down and the approaching summer gave opportunities for recreation. Off duty, the pilots had a choice between rough shooting and sailing one of the two 12ft dinghies which had been chartered from the Pembroke Yacht Club. The enemy was not being very co-operative, however. It was suspected that the crews of the Ju 88s which penetrated the area had learned how to pick up fighter control broadcasts and take avoiding action. The squadron therefore sought out the Junkers at source by attacking Lannion and Morlaix airfields. During one of these sorties, on 23 July 1942, they lost two of their aircraft, their first operational casualties since December 1941.

In August, No. 263 Squadron moved on to Colerne near Bath, where its aircraft were to be fitted with bomb racks to see out their remaining operational life in the intruder role rather than as interceptor fighters.

The next occupants of Angle were No. 152 (Hyderabad) Squadron, armed with Spitfires. They arrived on 16 August and the intensity of operations required of the station can be illustrated by the fact that on the very next day they flew patrols continuously from 0530 to 2130. First blood was drawn on 23 August when a Ju 88 was shot down; it landed south of Waterford. On 26 August two of their aircraft were lost, apparently having collided with each other over the sea in bad weather. On 30 September the squadron left Angle, destined for North Africa.

The next squadron did not arrive until 26 October. It was No. 421 Squadron of the Royal Canadian Air Force and it stayed until the end of January 1943, flying the usual convoy protection patrols. They also, like their predecessors, lost two aircraft in a collision, this time near the airfield. One crashed in the sea off Thorne Point and the pilot was able to swim ashore; the other went in on the airfield. In a very brave act the NAAFI manager, Mr. Poole, got the pilot out of the wreckage just before it blew up, but he died before reaching hospital.

The departure of No. 421 Squadron was effectively the end of Angle as an operational station. No. 412 Squadron moved in for a month and, between its leaving and the transfer of the airfield to the Admiralty on 1 May 1943, Angle saw only a short exercise of airborne forces gliders and a test of one of Dr. Barnes Wallis' experimental bouncing bombs.

6. 1943
Pembroke Dock
Talbenny
Dale
St. David's

Pembroke Dock's comparatively quiet period was to end in 1943. The renewed intensity of the station's battle with the U boats was not to let up again until the war was won.

The submarine war was anything but static. Geography and technology brought changes, which affected both the strategy and the tactics of the battle. The first big change was in 1940, when the whole coastline of western Europe came under German control, ports on the Biscay coast becoming available to their submarines, thus shortening their passage to the south-western approaches. Shipping losses increased, and the submarines surfaced mainly at night. The sighting of a submarine periscope in daylight was difficult and, although a surfaced boat could be detected at night by the 1.5 metre wavelength radar then in use, attack was almost impossible; an aircraft could hope to make an attacking run only with the help of the illuminating reflection of a full moon on the surface of the sea.

Two innovations changed the situation. Those Wellington aircraft which were fitted with forward-looking radar were provided with a searchlight - the

Leigh light - which, if switched on when a surfaced submarine was about a mile ahead, gave conditions something like daylight. This device came into use in June 1942; by August, U boats in the Bay were having to change their tactics and surface to charge their batteries by day when they stood more chance of seeing approaching aircraft. This increased the number of daylight sightings and attacks. However, it was not long before the Germans were able to detect the 1.5 metre radar and in the winter of 1942-43, when they were able to revert to night surfacing, shipping losses went up once more.

The next development in this war of technology was the introduction of 10cm wavelength ASV radar, using an aerial which swept through 360 degrees. Its detection range was about four times as great as that of the earlier equipment, and even if a its presence was detected by a U boat, the sweeping of the search beam made it impossible for the enemy to know whether or not it was the object of the aircraft's interest. The effect of this was to make it dangerous once more for German U boats to surface at night, and by mid-1943 they were again forced to take the difficult choice of coming up by day. As a result submarines in transit through the Bay could expect, on average, to be sighted twice.

Given the ability of the submarine to submerge and the vagaries of the Atlantic weather, whether or not a sighting could lead to attack was one matter, but the strain on submarine crews was another, and it was greatly increased as long as air cover of the Bay could be maintained at a high intensity. The U boats were driven to operating in packs and attempting to fight it out with attacking aircraft on the surface. The patrolling of the Bay by German fighter aircraft in order to drive off the Coastal Command forces was also stepped up, but the initiative had come over to the Allied side and when the next technological advance appeared in the form of the Schnorkel tube, it was too late to swing the balance back.

It is against this background of factors that the changing fortunes of the anti-submarine forces have to be judged.

The operational lives of Talbenny and Dale were now limited; No. 304 Squadron was to leave on 2 April 1943 and No. 311 on 27 May, and they were not replaced by anti-submarine squadrons. The Wellingtons recorded two attacks in January, the only sightings of the enemy and both by No. 304 Squadron. On 26th January sixteen aircraft of both squadrons made a bombing attack on Bordeaux harbour. A No. 304 Squadron aircraft had an intriguing encounter on 21 January when it came upon a black, twin-engined, twin-tailed flying boat off Fastnet Rock with no identification markings; it dived away in the direction of Eire.

February, March and April 1943 were also fairly quiet months, with few highlights to break the tedium of long patrols. Before leaving for Beaulieu to convert to Liberator aircraft, No. 311 Squadron recorded a successful attack on a surfaced U boat; it earned the congratulations of the A O C in C Coastal Command, Air Marshal Sir John Slessor, for having the highest assessment in the Command both for day and for night operations in the quarter from December 1942 to February 1943.

No. 304 Squadron also had some U boat attacks to record, and more brushes with enemy fighters including the formidable FW 190. One of its Wellingtons fought four Ju 88s for an hour and, in spite of suffering extensive damage, saw them off. It was not the Junkers' lucky day as they ran into a Beaufighter patrol and three of them were destroyed.

An indication of the work of the Wellingtons can be gained from a breakdown of the flying hours of No. 304 Squadron for February: 484 hours on anti-submarine patrol, 76 on bombing operations against German occupied ports, 14 on convoy escort and 13 hours on general reconnaissance. At this time No. 19 Group calculated that throughout its area there were on average four submarine sightings a day, at a cost of sixty flying hours each. Whether a sighting was turned into a successful attack or not, the total effect in making life difficult for the U boats was obvious. In addition, they had to contend with the work of the anti-submarine vessels of the Royal Navy, and further back Bomber Command was bombing the U boat bases, construction and repair yards, factories and communications, all of which significantly reduced the number of boats able to put to sea at all.

1943 opened at Pembroke Dock with Nos. 119 and 210 Squadrons in residence, patrolling the No. 19 Group area, but they did not stay much longer. In April No. 210 Squadron was moved to Hamworthy (Poole Harbour) and No. 119 Squadron was, for the time being, disbanded and its Sunderlands dispersed to other units. This was as a result of a new policy which increased the number of aircraft in General Reconnaissance squadrons from six to nine, plus three in immediate reserve.

These two squadrons were replaced by the return of No. 228, long associated with Pembroke Dock, and No. 461 Squadron, Royal Australian Air Force, both with Sunderlands. These enlarged squadrons, together with No. 308 Ferry Training Unit which had been formed at Pembroke Dock in March 1943, and Nos. 11 and 12 Flying Boat Fitting Units, combined to make the Haven a very busy anchorage, with taxying aircraft dodging among those already moored. On occasions almost a hundred flying boats were present. The two Flying Boat Fitting Units were busy modifying, fitting out and testing aircraft. Moorings were to the north of the station, flying boats also being dispersed along the banks of the river to the east. The actual touch-down area was some two miles to the west. The instructions issued to pilots will give some measure of their problems:

"Taxi into harbour until the town of Milford is passed. When past Milford keep to the buoyed channel to the northern side of the estuary as extensive mud flats lie to the south. Past the south side chequered buoy at Wear Point turn NE so as to round the starboard buoys off Spit. Taxying from the night flying flare path opposite Angle Bay is difficult without local knowledge and it is advisable for visiting pilots to do so only when guided by an RAF pinnace or seaplane tender. Weather permitting, aircraft may be moored at RAF buoys on each side of the estuary opposite Angle Bay."

The new arrivals quickly settled down. A week after the arrival of No. 461 Squadron one of its aircraft attacked a surfaced U boat off Cape Finisterre. It was last seen up on end, heading vertically down.

May 1943 was No. 461 Squadron's best month since its formation, sighting eight U boats, sinking one and attacking several others. The crews also experienced increased enemy air activity, with a number of attacks by Ju 88s; one Sunderland attacked by four suffered many hits and another, attacked by six, absorbed nearly two hundred holes from bullets and cannon shells. One sample sortie report recorded five Spanish fishing vessels, one U boat and four Ju 88s.

On 26 May 1943 a Sunderland was lost in an attempt to land at sea to rescue the occupants of a dinghy. The aircrew themselves then spent fourteen hours in their dinghy before being picked up by another aircraft and transferred to a destroyer. The rescuing aircraft, taking off again in a high swell, sustained a hole seven feet by four feet in its hull. This brought about a unique feat when the captain, Flying Officer Singleton, landed his Sunderland on Angle aerodrome without further damage.

June 1943 opened with a successful attack on a U boat by a No. 228 Squadron Sunderland, assisted by another patrolling Sunderland and a Whitley. On its way home the No. 228 Squadron aircraft met another U boat, but having no remaining depth charges the crew had to be satisfied with a machine gun attack, which at least forced the U boat to submerge.

No. 461 Squadron sank no U boats in June, but on 2nd one of its aircraft put up a fight which was described by the Chief of the Air Staff as "an epic battle which will go down in history as one of the finest instances in this war of the triumph of coolness, skill and determination against overwhelming odds." It is worth describing in some detail.

The Captain of Sunderland 461/N, EJ 134, was Flight Lieutenant Walker and his crew were Pilot Officers Dowling, Amiss and Simpson, Flight Sergeants Fuller, Miller and Goode and Sergeants Miles, Turner, Lane and Watson. Miles and Fuller were British, the rest Australian.

At seven o'clock in the evening of 2 June, while flying at 2,000 feet, they sighted eight Ju 88s on the port quarter and a thousand feet above them. The

Ju 88s formed up for attack, three on each beam and 1,500 feet above and one on each quarter, 1,500 yards away. The Sunderland jettisoned its bombs to lighten its load. In the first attack by the Ju 88s on each beam the Sunderland's port outer engine was set on fire; this was extinguished but the engine was no longer useable. The pilot's steering compass was also hit, igniting the alcohol in the bowl which set the captain's clothing alight. The first pilot took over while this was dealt with. The enemy aircraft made at least twenty attacks of the same type, the Sunderland taking evasive action.

One Ju 88, after attacking from the starboard beam, passed over the midships gunner who shot it down at point blank range. The mid and nose gunners then shot down a second Ju 88 attacking from the port side; a third was shot down by the mid and tail gunners as it came in on the port quarter.

The five remaining Ju 88s continued to attack. One was hit by the nose gunner, breaking off with its port engine on fire and with smoke pouring from its cockpit. Every one of the enemy aircraft was damaged. The Sunderland's hull was holed in many places and the tail turret hydraulics, the rudder and elevator trimming wires, the radio and communication systems were all damaged. The port outer engine seized up and its propeller fell off.

During a climbing attack from the starboard quarter the starboard galley gunner, Sergeant Miles, was hit in the stomach and leg and died twenty minutes later. The navigator was wounded in the leg and the rear gunner knocked unconscious during violent evasive action. The engagement ended at 7.45pm when the two enemy aircraft still in the fight broke away to the east having presumably run short of fuel and ammunition. The Sunderland, nearly all its ammunition gone, set course roughly for home using its dinghy radio for communications. It beached at Marazion (near Penzance).

Sergeant Miles was buried at Pembroke Dock. Flight Lieutenant Walker was awarded the DSO, Pilot Officer Simpson the DFC and Flight Sergeants Goode and Fuller DFMs.

On 4 June 1943 the A O C in C of Coastal Command visited Pembroke Dock accompanied by HRH The Duke of Gloucester.

On 14 June 1943 a Sunderland of No. 228 Squadron sighted three U boats in company; two submerged immediately, the third as the Sunderland attacked. Some Ju 88s in the vicinity showed a considerable degree of circumspection, which was hardly surprising after the experience of their fellows at the hands of Walker and his crew. It was an isolated incident however and in July a Sunderland of No. 228 Squadron fell victim to a patrol of similar aircraft.

In July the patrols had more experience of the enemy tactic of remaining on the surface to engage them with gunfire. In one such incident a *Sunderland* fought with a pack of three U boats off the north coast of Spain, sinking one of them.

No. 461 Squadron sighted seven U boats in the month, resulting in three attacks and one definite sinking. They also brought about the rescue of survivors at sea on two occasions, one involving a group of seven dinghies containing about fifty men. On 30 July there was a notable battle in which three U boats were engaged by aircraft of five different squadrons, including Nos. 228 and 461, and the Second Escort Group, Royal Navy. All were sunk, one probably by the No. 461 Squadron participant, but not before giving a very good account of themselves, driving off several of their attackers.

July also saw the arrival at Pembroke Dock of the amphibian PBY 5s of VP 63, a patrol squadron of the United States Navy. Their equipment was interesting in that they were the first aircraft to be fitted with the Magnetic Anomaly Detector, designed to locate the magnetic field of a submarine's hull. The detection could only be made when the aircraft was over the vessel, making a conventional attack impossible. The PBYs were therefore each armed with thirty retro-bombs which, on release, were propelled backwards to cancel the forward speed imparted by the aircraft so that they dropped vertically. This sophisticated weapons system was not very successful as such but the squadron flew 449 patrol missions before leaving Pembroke Dock in December, outperforming the Sunderland squadrons in hours flown and making a large contribution to the interdiction of the Bay. VP 63 lost only one aircraft during its stay, shot down by Ju 88s on an early patrol, but they were able to claim two certain and one probable enemy aircraft in return; this was the first engagement between US Naval Aviation and the German Air Force.

When they left Pembroke Dock the PBYs went to Port Lyautey in Morocco where their detection equipment proved effective in obstructing the passage of the narrow Straits of Gibraltar to U boats.

At the end of July the A O C in C was able to record that "the British and American squadrons in the United Kingdom have between them during July broken all records and have shown that the enemy cannot hope to get away with it by passing through the Bay in packs and fighting back on the surface." The battle of the Bay was all but won.

The first engagement recorded in August was between a surfaced U boat and a No. 228 Squadron aircraft, both being damaged. The next day a submarine was destroyed in a fight with two Sunderlands, one each from Nos. 228 and 461.

Enemy aircraft were still very active in the Bay. On 15 August a No. 461 Squadron aircraft was fortunate to survive a battle with four Ju 88s in which it was badly damaged, one of the crew being killed and another wounded. Two other No. 461 Squadron Sunderlands were shot down by packs of Ju 88s.

The experiences of the submarines in surface battles once more dictated a change of tactics in that they only surfaced in the dark and the Pembroke Dock aircraft had no more sightings for the rest of the year; their success in keeping the enemy boats down was however as effective if not as spectacular as the battles with gun and depth charge. Air engagements continued; in one instance in September a fight as fierce as that of 2 June took place when Flight Lieutenant Marrows and his crew, of No. 461 Squadron, engaged six Ju 88s for nearly an hour, and three of the Sunderland's engines and all but one of its guns were put out of action. The Ju 88s were damaged, one probably being destroyed, before the Sunderland had to ditch and its crew, several of them wounded, were obliged to take to their dinghies. Another No. 461 Squadron Sunderland was destroyed in one of the other engagements.

Unusual operations in the last quarter of 1943 included an order from Coastal Command to a No. 461 Squadron aircraft to attack two Spanish trawlers with gunfire. There was no explanation and the trawlers were fired on until they put out white flags. This was an isolated incident, although it was common practice to drop warning leaflets on these boats.

In December 1943, aircraft of Nos. 228 and 461 Squadrons took part in a successful operation against surface ships in the Bay. Thanks to their skill in shadowing and directing, an enemy merchant ship was sunk by a British submarine and three destroyers were sunk, and another damaged, by other ships of the Royal Navy.

There was an organisational change at Pembroke Dock. Angle airfield, which had been transferred to the Admiralty on 1 May, was on 7 September returned to the RAF and put under the control of Pembroke Dock, so that all night flying in the Haven area could be co-ordinated, as Angle Bay was in use as a dispersed flying boat flare path. No. 304 Squadron, which had moved to Cornwall from Dale, had to use Angle for night flying because of difficulties at its home base.

The move of Nos. 304 and 311 Squadrons from Pembrokeshire was compensated, later in the year, by new arrivals. Royal Air Force St. Davids was opened on 26 August 1943 under the command of Group Captain H V Drew, OBE AFC, in No. 19 Group. The airfield was not fit for occupation until the end of November, when No. 517 Squadron arrived to operate there until its intended home at Brawdy was completed. No. 517 was a meterological reconnaissance squadron equipped with eighteen Halifax V aircraft, plus six in immediate reserve. The squadron had previously been equipped with Hampdens and Flying Fortresses and so its first task was to work up with its new machines.

The squadrons meant for St. Davids were Nos. 58 and 502, both also equipped with Halifaxes. Until the airfield was fit for operations, in early

December, they were based at Holmsley South (Hampshire). Their function was to patrol the Bay of Biscay contributing to the air cover, although they were bombers rather than specialised anti-submarine aircraft. Nevertheless they attacked submarines on two occasions in December, and also a convoy of merchant ships and destroyers off northern Spain on Christmas Eve. The three squadrons at St. Davids at the end of 1943 represented the total strength of Halifax aircraft in the Command.

During 1943 there was a brief addition to the airfields of Pembrokeshire. Exercise Jantzen was a rehearsal in Carmarthen Bay of the landing and maintenance of an assault force over beaches, and one requirement was an airstrip for close air support. The Royal Engineers set to work at Cyffig, near Tavernspite, on 24 July using Sommerfield tracking. At 1630 on 26 July a Mustang came in for the first landing. The umpires decided that the Royal Engineers would have to do better than that when they got to Normandy.

7. Ground Radar

The operation of aircraft and shipping under war conditions, and the defence of the area, called for a comprehensive radar network. At Warren, near Castlemartin, Hayscastle Cross and Folly, near Roch, the 325ft transmitter towers of the long range CH (Chain Home) early warning stations stood over the countryside.

CHL (Chain Home Low) stations for the detection of low flying aircraft and the surveillance of the sea surface were sited at Strumble Head, St. David's Head, St. Twynnels, Kete and Old Castle Head. A GCI (Ground Control Interception) radar for the direction of fighter aircraft operated at Ripperstone near Talbenny. Other equipments for detecting the height of aircraft, for navigation and for communication were to be found at the same sites or near them.

The radars were linked to reporting centres, at Milford Haven for surface shipping, and through Rhossili, Swansea and centres across the Bristol Channel for warning of approaching aircraft.

Beside their prime task of plotting and directing aircraft and shipping, the radar stations were able to provide a searchlight system which was of great value to friendly aircraft in poor weather conditions, by laying their light beams in the direction of the nearest airfield.

After the breakout of the Allied forces in Normandy, and the neutralisation of the German air bases in France, the importance of the Pembrokeshire radar system began progressively to diminish. In August 1944 the CHL at St. Twynnels closed and in September the homing searchlights were removed from Warren and Hayscastle Cross. By January 1945 the CH at Warren was scheduled for dismantling and, in February and March, Warren and Strumble Head ceased their surface tracking functions. Hayscastle Cross became non-operational in May and in June the surface tracking room at Milford Haven closed down.

Folly and Hayscastle Cross CH stations were revived for a short while in the early 1950s, in the aftermath of the Korean War, until their function was taken over by new and more advanced radars.

8. 1944

Pembroke Dock
St. Davids
Brawdy

1944 was the year of climax, when events built up to the invasion, and tension decreased as German resistance crumbled. Coastal Command in the No. 19 Group area of operations experienced the full effect of the process. The year opened with appalling weather at the bases and the accustomed routine of Biscay patrols.

Weather was bad in the Bay also and the difficulties of bombing small targets at sea reduced the effectiveness of the aircraft, especially of the Halifaxes. Nevertheless they made frequent contacts, ten sightings in January including one in which the pilot, Flying Officer Spurgeon of No. 502 Squadron attempted to compensate for poor visibility by making what must have been the first, if not the only, dive bombing attack by a Halifax, but with uncertain effect.

The flying boats were also recording sightings but the enemy's defensive tactics kept down the number of attacks. On 17 January 1944 a Sunderland of No. 228 Squadron came down in St. George's Channel and sank. The crew were able to take to their dinghies, from which they were picked up by a fast minelayer and landed at Tenby.

At the end of January 1944, No. 461 Squadron's patrol area was moved from the Bay to the area of Fastnet Rock off the south west coast of Ireland, in order to protect the increasing military convoy traffic from America. They immediately lived up to their motto, "They shall not pass", by sinking their first U boat for six months. Otherwise they had few sightings, although on one occasion they brought about the rescue of United States aircrew from three dinghies.

Once they had settled down with their new aircraft, No. 517 Squadron's routine consisted of long flights of eleven hours or so, mainly towards the south, following various pressure levels to help build up the weather forecasts which were so important to air operations generally, and which specifically played such a vital role in the last stages of the invasion planning. They sometimes landed at Gibraltar on two-way reconnaissance flights.

As the investigation of weather conditions was its job, it is not surprising that the weather itself was one of No. 517 Squadron's main hazards. In February 1944 it moved to its intended base at Brawdy, leaving Nos. 58 and 502 Squadrons at St. Davids but the two airfields were operated in close co-operation; since their runways were in different directions, they could be used to best advantage according to wind conditions. The longer runways at Brawdy were also used by the St. Davids aircraft for taking off with heavier fuel loads and armament than their own airfield would allow.

February, March and April 1944 produced little anti-submarine action although in March No. 19 Group broke all previous records for operational flying hours, No. 228 Squadron being singled out for special praise. The patrols were producing their desired effect. Enemy surface ships were met from time to time, and in March a Halifax attacked a formation of seven E boats, coming off the worst with eighty-seven shrapnel holes from the ships' anti-aircraft guns. There were other unwelcome events in the quarter. In February a Halifax was shot down by Ju 88s over St. Bride's Bay, and in March another crashed into the sea off St. David's Head with the loss of its crew of eight. Also in March a No. 461 Squadron aircraft was shot down and another badly damaged in battles with Ju 88s.

In preparation for the invasion in which the No. 19 Group operational area would be so vital, No. 201 Squadron was in April deployed to Pembroke Dock from Castle Archdale (Co. Fermanagh) with new Sunderland Mk II aircraft. The Sunderland had been steadily improved as experience and technology developed. Now its operational equipment was based on the ASV Mk III centimetric radar; for navigation it had Gee Mk II, a Distant Reading Compass and a radio altimeter; for attack a Mk III Low Level Bombsight, eight 250lb Mk XI Torpex depth charges and up to eighty 1.7in illuminating flares. For defence it had fifteen guns: four fixed Browning 303s and one .5 firing forward together with a further two Browning 303s in a Frazer Nash 5 nose turret; two more 303s were in the mid upper turret and four in the tail turret; in addition one Vickers Gas Operated free gun was available on each side in the amidships galley area. Typical squadron equipment was now twelve machines with two more in immediate reserve.

There was a continuing lull in submarine activity as the forces of both sides prepared and waited for the test to come, and during the first days of June 1944 the squadrons rested.

By D-Day they were at their task of sealing off the approaches to the Channel, in order to protect the route of the invasion fleet and its lines of communication. The complex pattern of patrol boxes worked out by Coastal Command ensured that every point from the southern coast of Eire to the Biscay coast of the Brest peninsula was under ASV survey every thirty minutes.

The orders to the U boat commanders were that every Allied vessel in the invasion forces should be attacked regardless of risk. In the event, the air and surface anti-submarine forces were so effective that in the month of June not one cross-Channel ship was lost to a U boat, in spite of their determined efforts to get through, both submerged and by fighting on the surface, and by the use of radar decoys and the newly-developed Schnorkel tubes. During the month, No. 19 Group made no fewer than fifty-seven attacks on U boats, and its Halifaxes bombed harbours of refuge in the Channel Islands. The coastal aircraft were greatly helped by the fact that they were working under the umbrella of complete air superiority which kept off their opponents, the Ju 88s and FW 190s.

Pembroke Dock played an important role in this effort; No. 201 Squadron flew seventy-one sorties, fifty-five of them in the peak period between the 9 and 25 June, recording their first success in their first sortie after H-Hour. Flight Lieutenant Baverstock DFC DFM and his crew fought a gun battle with their adversary before sinking it with six depth charges.

No. 228 Squadron flew seventy-seven sorties, sighting four U boats and two enemy surface vessels; three of the U boats were attacked with promising effect.

There was a price: No. 228 Squadron lost two of its best crews; No. 201 lost one captained by a Flight Commander, Squadron Leader W.D.B. Rutter DFC and Bar, in a battle with a surfaced submarine. No. 461 Squadron also lost a Sunderland but the crew were rescued.

By the end of June most of the enemy submarines still afloat had had to return to port. In July only one sinking was recorded by Pembroke Dock, to the account of No. 201 Squadron. In the month the U boats succeeded in sinking their first ship serving the beach heads.

August brought a further change. The breakout of the American forces on the right flank of the invasion front intensified patrol activity along the Channel coast, especially in daylight, to prevent the escape of enemy shipping from Brest, Lorient and St. Nazaire. Enemy submarines were also at sea in strength as their pens were threatened by the land advance. The Sunderland squadrons all exceeded a thousand hours on patrol in the month. Another U boat fell to Flight Lieutenant Baverstock and his crew, of No. 201 Squadron; No. 461 sank two more, bringing their total to seven certainties and four damaged; No. 228 Squadron attacked three. As the enemy air force in western France was now defeated, the patrolling aircraft could operate close to the coast further down the Bay, below the mouth of the Gironde, looking for enemy shipping retreating to the south. On 5 August one Halifax sighted no fewer than ten minesweepers and two Sperrbreckers moving between the Ile de Groix, off Lorient, and the mainland and on 13 August another caught three

U boats and four minesweepers entering the mouth of the Gironde; in its attack the Halifax was severely damaged and the rear gunner was killed.

However, enemy activity on this coast did not last long; the invasion of the French Mediterranean coast was a further blow to the German forces, reducing their room for manoeuvre. By mid-August crews were able to take some leave for the first time since April and No. 58 Squadron left St. Davids, to be followed four weeks later by No. 502. St. Davids had been completed just in time for the invasion. By this time however the focus of interest was transferred to the northern seas and the Norwegian coast, but the need for weather forecasting did not diminish, and No. 517 Squadron remained at Brawdy until the war was finally over.

On 18 August HRH The Duke of Gloucester, who was Governor General designate of Australia, visited No. 461 Squadron at Pembroke Dock.

The remaining operational activity from Pembroke Dock was concentrated to the south of Ireland, where shipping from the United States in support of their land forces was still to be found and the U boats were able once more to operate with Schnorkel in shallow waters. This area was under the control of No. 15 Group which directed the patrols. No. 201 Squadron returned to Castle Archdale in October, and other Pembroke Dock boats were to be found operating in the north on detachment to Scottish and Shetland bases.

No. 201 Squadron was replaced by Pembroke Dock's first Canadian unit, No. 422 RCAF Squadron, which arrived with Sunderlands from Castle Archdale on 4 November. They settled quickly into the routine of their new operational area and just as quickly into the social life of Pembroke Dock, introducing the inhabitants into the mysteries of square dancing at St. Patrick's Church Hall and later at Trinity Hall. This was rechristened "Canada House", and was complete with murals of "an airman's dream", which by that time was turning towards home and beauty.

9. 1945 and the End   Pembroke Dock

In January 1945 No. 461 Squadron was unfortunate enough to lose three aircraft in a gale, which drove a large motor vessel on to two of them at their moorings, and a baulk of timber on to the third. The only operational loss was one of No. 228's aircraft which crashed in an attempt to sink a U boat at Schnorkel depth.

8 May 1945 was VE Day and the Admiralty broadcast orders to U boats to surface, report their positions and fly a white or a black flag. The first to be seen was U 249, by an aircraft of No. 228 Squadron; No. 461 sighted three more. There were no instances of submarines continuing to fight.

The end was to come quickly for Pembroke Dock squadrons. On 3 June No. 228 Squadron was informed that it was to be disbanded next day. No. 461 was disbanded on 20th and No. 422 flew its aircraft to Castle Archdale for disposal before the crews left for Bassingbourne (Cambridgeshire) to convert to Liberators in Transport Command. Canada was beginning to prepare for the Anglo-Canadian air force - Tiger Force - which was being formed to join the Pacific war.

Coastal Command now began to re-group into a peacetime deployment, in which Pembroke Dock played a part for a while. Of the operational squadrons, No. 201 came back on 2 August 1945, staying until 30 April 1946. Early in 1949 the only remaining home-based flying boat squadrons, Nos. 201 and 230, moved into Pembroke Dock from Calshot where the shipping in Southampton Water had become too congested for their safety. They exercised from other war-time anchorages and carried out tasks for which the land-based Shackeltons were not suited, one being the support of scientific expeditions to Greenland.

On 28 February 1957 the two remaining boat squadrons disbanded and Pembroke Dock's career in military aviation was ended. The base was put on care and maintenance on 31 March 1957, and handed back to the Admiralty on 31 March 1959.

V - COASTAL COMMAND NON-OPERATIONAL UNITS

1. Haverfordwest and Templeton

As the Royal Air Force units based in Pembrokeshire were primarily engaged in maritime reconnaissance and anti-submarine operations, most non-operational activities were geared to their support.

Some of this work occupied two airfields which never accommodated operational squadrons; Haverfordwest (or Withybush), and Templeton. They were developed as a pair, Haverfordwest being the main base with Templeton as its satellite. Their construction was bedevilled by delay and when, on 30 November 1942, the first four Whitley aircraft arrived at Haverfordwest as the advance guard of No. 3 (Coastal) Operational Training Unit the crews found that the airfield was a quagmire and without hangars; there were also serious problems with the electricity supply. They left immediately and on 17 December the Senior Officer in charge of Administration of No. 17 (Training) Group complained that "labour and plant are continually withdrawn from Haverfordwest to the stations under construction at Brawdy and St. Davids. The condition of the airfield at Haverfordwest can only be described as deplorable. A very limited amount of day flying can take place at

Templeton if the weather is good and with experienced pilots". It was obviously no good for training but as it was capable of limited use the Station Headquarters of the pair was set up at Templeton on 7 January 1943 to administer No. 306 Ferry Training Unit which moved on to Northern Ireland in June, when No. 3 OTU was at last able to move into Haverfordwest.

No. 3 (Coastal) OTU had the task of training complete crews in general reconnaissance skills. It was equipped with Whitleys, soon to be replaced by Wellingtons, and with Ansons, based at Templeton which had no night landing facilities. The unit's life was short as on 4 January 1944 it was disbanded and absorbed into No. 6 OTU at Silloth (Cumberland). No. 7 OTU, with a similar role, moved in from Northern Ireland to take its place but by May it was redesignated No. 4 Refresher Flying Unit, equipped with Wellington Mk X and XI aircraft and later Liberators and Halifaxes. This unit's career was short, too, and it was disbanded on 5 October 1944.

There was then a gap until 1 January 1945 when No. 8 (Coastal) OTU moved into Haverfordwest with one flight at Templeton. This unit trained crews for photographic reconnaissance which, although carried out by Spitfires and Mosquitoes, was a Coastal Command responsibility. It had a secondary task of making a photographic survey of Great Britain. The flight at Templeton did not stay long, moving to Brawdy on 27 February. Templeton was now virtually closed and its equipment was being disposed of. It did some repair work for No. 8 OTU until that unit left Haverfordwest on 21 June 1945.

The last units at Haverfordwest were Nos. 20 and 21 Air Crew Holding Units. These accommodated reinforcement aircrews from the Commonwealth Air Training Scheme, many of whom did not reach operational squadrons before the end of hostilities. When the ACHUs moved to Thorney Island (Sussex), Haverfordwest was handed over to the Ministry of Civil Aviation on 1 December 1945.

2. Coastal Command Development Unit   Carew Cheriton
                                          Dale
                                          Angle

Even if the Coastal Command career of Haverfordwest and Templeton was not very distinguished, three other airfields in the county housed a very important function of the Command at different times.

The Coastal Command Development Unit was formed at Carew Cheriton in December 1940. Its role was to carry out service trials of all radar equipment in use, or likely to be introduced, for general reconnaissance and to examine and develop tactics for its employment.

Its original equipment at Carew was one Hudson, one Beaufort and one Whitley but it was not long before the value of the unit was recognised, when its scope was increased to cover the service trials of all Coastal Command aircraft and equipment. A flying boat section was set up at Pembroke Dock, and aircraft were borrowed for trials while attached there for maintenance.

In January 1941 the unit was carrying out searchlight trials for anti-submarine attacks at night, for which they were allotted two Wellingtons, and in February they acquired a Beaufighter. The aircraft establishment continued to adapt to the requirements of the trials in hand.

Much of the work was concerned with ASV radar, and airborne trials took the form of homing on to lightships and small cargo vessels in the Bristol Channel as these were thought to give similar returns to partially submerged submarines. By January 1941 such ships were being detected at a range of six miles, and attack procedures for conditions of poor visibility were being worked out as well as blind bombing, wind finding and formation tactics using the ASV radar.

In November 1941 CCDU moved from Carew Cheriton to Northern Ireland. In April 1943 it returned to Pembrokeshire, this time to Dale, where it carried on its work until the airfield was transferred to the Admiralty on 7 September 1943, when the unit moved to Angle. It always had a heavy programme of work and between leaving Carew Cheriton and December 1943 it completed some two hundred major trials and many subsidiary tasks, supplying a vast amount of information and expertise to add to the efficiency of the operational squadrons.

3. No. 4 Armament Practice Camp   Carew Cheriton
    Talbenny

In November 1941 Carew Cheriton became the home of No. 4 Armament Practice Camp, equipped with a flight of Lysanders. This unit provided facilities for bombing and air-to-air firing practice for crews of Coastal Command squadrons, and also for Liberator squadrons of the United States Navy. It moved to Talbenny at the end of 1943 where it continued to fly Lysanders, with the addition of Martinets, staying until it was disbanded on 1 September 1945.

4. Non-Operational Flying Boat Units   Pembroke Dock

For a period, Pembroke Dock housed No. 308 Ferry Training Unit which was formed there in March 1943 and stayed until January 1944, when it moved to Oban. Its role was to train flying boat crews for the ferrying of their aircraft to overseas theatres.

There were also, necessarily, units concerned with the equipping and maintenance of the boats. Nos. 11 and 12 Flying Boat Fitting Units dealt with modifications and subsequent testing, while No. 3 Flying Boat Servicing Unit handled the regular inspections.

After the run down of flying boats at the end of the war, No. 4 Operational Training Unit moved down from Alnes (Cromarty Firth) when that base closed in August 1946. It stayed until July 1947, when it moved to Calshot and was renamed No. 235 OTU.

As flying boats differed so much from land-based aircraft, specialist instruction had to be maintained and a small Flying Boat Training Squadron was set up in October 1953, continuing until its disbandment in October 1956. By this time the remaining Sunderlands were nearly twenty years old, and no replacement was under development. The land-based Shackeltons, together with the flexibility provided by helicopters, satisfied the maritime reconnaissance requirement.

VI - UNITS OUTSIDE COASTAL COMMAND

1. Anti-Aircraft Cooperation - RAF Manorbier
Carew Cheriton

Target towing and the flying of radio controlled target aircraft - Tiger Moth 'Queen Bees' - took place from a strip at Manorbier from the mid-1930s. Starting with the summer training season of 1937, they were joined by a flight of No. 1 Anti-Aircraft Cooperation Unit towing targets. The pilotless aircraft were always available; when the airstrip was unserviceable they could be fitted with floats and, after being fired off the cliff top, landed on the water to be picked up by a salvage vessel and returned to Manorbier by road from Tenby.

Though the Manorbier grass field continued in use, B Flight of No. 1 AACU was based at Carew Cheriton. It was reorganised in November 1942 and the Carew component became No. 1607 Target Towing Flight, Nos.1608 and 1609 being at Aberporth. No. 1607 continued to work with the School of Anti-Aircraft Artillery at Manorbier.

Late in 1943 the provision was increased for a while by a detachment of C Flight of No. 595 Squadron, moved from Aberporth to Carew Cheriton and equipped with a Hawker Henley and some Miles Martinets. They towed targets at high level for the larger AA guns; they also made low approaches for the Bofors guns, and against British and United States naval vessels exercising off the Smalls. Two Hawker Hurricanes, also used for simulated low level attacks, operated from Manorbier until winter weather made this impracticable. One Hurricane, piloted by Sergeant Mwroka of the Polish Air Force, crashed into Heywood Lodge, Tenby after engine failure.

2. Naval Land Based Flying Units   Dale

When Dale was taken over by the Admiralty in September 1943 it became for a short while, until November, the home of No. 794 Squadron, Fleet Air Arm, which towed targets with Defiants, Fulmars, Masters and Martinets.

Dale was also used by operational squadrons as a base for training in army support and ground attack, roles which carrier-borne aircraft were expected to undertake in support of seaborne landings, until land based aircraft could be established ashore. Squadrons of No. 4 Naval Fighter Wing with Spitfire and Seafire aircraft, whose parent ships were the escort carriers Hunter, Stalker and Attacker, trained at Dale in February and March 1944 before going to the Mediterranean. They later went on to the Far East to provide air cover for the assault on Rangoon in May 1945, reaching Singapore in time to witness the Japanese surrender on 12 September.

In April 1944, No. 790 Squadron was based at Dale, providing aircraft for the fighter direction school at Kete. From February 1946 No. 784 Squadron carried out night fighter training, merging with No. 790 Squadron in October 1946. No.790 remained at Dale until the station closed down in December 1947.

3. Carew Cheriton as a Training Station

No. 254 Squadron having left Carew Cheriton on 24 July 1942, the station was transferred from No. 19 Group, Coastal Command to No. 25 Group, Flying Training Command. Although it remained for the time being the home of No. 4 Armament Practice Camp and the AA Target Towing Flight it did not, in the event, become a flying training station. Instead, in October 1942, it was transferred to Technical Training Command to accommodate a radio school.

No. 10 Radio School at Carew Cheriton was equipped with some twenty Oxfords, to which Ansons were added in January 1943. The unit trained air wireless operators until it was disbanded in November 1945.

In February 1944 Wing Commander Ira Jones, one of the outstanding pilots of the Great War who also served in the Second, was asked by the local authorities to advise on the suitability of airfields for post-war civilian flying, including Carew Cheriton, but the base finally closed on 1 May 1946.

4. Rudbaxton

The airfield at Rudbaxton did not relate to the activities of the other airfields in Pembrokeshire, which were variously linked by operational or directly supporting commitments for an appreciable portion, if not for the whole, of their existence. Rudbaxton was a landing ground used for the storage of aircraft turned out by No. 38 Maintenance Unit at Llandow. In use from April 1941, it was not highly regarded because it did not have adequate facilities for uncertain weather. The Maintenance Unit ceased to use it in

September 1942, as Haverfordwest was becoming due for occupation and Rudbaxton was under its flight path.

5. Ferry Training
Templeton
Talbenny

While No. 308 Ferry Training Unit provided flying boat training at Pembroke Dock, there were similar units at nearby airfields for land based aircraft.

Templeton
In January 1943, No. 306 Ferry Training Unit was formed at Templeton to train Beaufort crews at the rate of twenty-five a month for ferrying these aircraft to reinforce overseas theatres. The first aircraft and crews were dispatched on 13 April, but the unit's productive life was short at this station as on 15 June it moved on to Northern Ireland.

Talbenny
When the operational squadrons had left Talbenny they were replaced, on 4 March 1943, by No. 303 Ferry Training Unit equipped with Wellingtons. The unit trained, and retained on its strength, ferry crews whose job it was to fly reinforcement aircraft out to overseas theatres, and also reinforcement crews who were to remain in the theatre to join operational squadrons with their aircraft. The unit dispatched forty to fifty aircraft each month, rising to a peak in the middle of 1944 of nearly eighty ferry crews and some ninety aircraft a month.

From July 1944, No. 3 Aircraft Dispatch Unit was based at Talbenny to collect machines from Aircraft Preparation Units; in October 1944 No. 303 FTU became No. 11 Ferry Unit for ferry preparation of overseas reinforcement aircraft of the Warwick, Wellington, Ventura and similar types. Also handled were Ansons, Oxfords, Spitfires and Dakotas. The nature of the work was much the same as before and No. 3 ADU merged with it. No. 11 Ferry Unit was disbanded on 15 August 1945, its work done.

RAF Talbenny, which had been in Transport Command since October 1943, was transferred on 25 March 1946 to Fighter Command, closing on 15 December 1946. It was later transferred back to Coastal Command, parented by Pembroke Dock, until 21 September 1950 but was inactive. On that date an MF/DF station, which became No. 104 Signals Unit, was formed there and remained until April 1945, when Talbenny once more became an inactive station in Coastal Command until it was finally disposed of on 1 November 1958.

6. Transport Conversion

St. Davids
Brawdy

Once St. Davids and Brawdy had lost their operational role, except for the meterological flights of No. 517 Squadron, they were made available for training and in October 1944 a detachment of No. 220 Squadron arrived from the Azores for conversion from Fortresses to Liberators. These large American bombers, which had been obtained under lease-lend, were allocated either to Coastal Command or to overseas theatres rather than to Bomber Command. The detachment returned to the Azores in December.

In June 1945 No. 53 Squadron moved with Liberators into St. Davids from Iceland, and No. 220 Squadron came back from the Azores to convert from their anti-submarine duties to the task of transporting troops out to the Pacific war. The squadrons were then to transfer to Transport Command. The crews dropped their gunners and extra pilots; wireless operators were taken in from the disbanded flying boat squadrons Nos. 210 and 228, and from Wellington crews.

The end of the war with Japan did not change the nature of their intended work, only its direction, as once they had been trained the squadrons left for Merrifield (Somerset) to set about the job of ferrying troops from the Far East back home.

With the completion of this training and the departure of No. 517 Squadron from Brawdy, the role of St. Davids and its satellite came to an end. St. Davids was reduced to care and maintenance and on 1 January 1946 Brawdy was transferred to the Admiralty, remaining a Royal Naval Air Station in support of the Aircraft Direction Centre at Kete until its transfer back to the Royal Air Force on 1 April 1971.

VII

The aircraft which took off from Pembrokeshire in both wars had a common purpose: the protection of shipping from submarine attack in the south-western approaches. If the airmen who flew on convoy escort in 1918 had been transported to 1939 they would have found little changed. Their machines would have been more reliable and would have stayed up longer but they would still have had to seek their quarry by staring at the water and, in the unlikely event of finding a U boat, their attacking speed would have been too low and their weapons inadequate.

The advances came later when better aircraft with greater armament were equipped with electronic aids to navigation and search. The U boats also developed, both in performance and in concealment, and a complex tactical battle was played out against a background of geography and technology.

It was hard fought by well matched but very different opponents. Both submariners and aircrew were volunteers who elected to serve in unnatural and hazardous environments, beneath the sea and in the air above. There was mutual respect but few if any would have exchanged roles. The flying boat crews themselves were a race apart even among fellow airmen - half sailor and able to read sea states and wind lanes to find their way.

Once hostilities were over the operational squadrons immediately dispersed, leaving only the remnants to follow more gradually. Australians, Canadians, Americans, Poles, Czechs, Dutch and above all the men and women from other parts of Britain, had here worked and fought, concerned with the war and the enemy rather than with their surroundings, and many had died.

The fighting ranged from close by to distant waters and targets. The success of the airmen was measured by the relatively free movement of shipping, arriving with food and supplies of all kinds and with reinforcement from America, and delivering safely the invasion forces for the liberation of Western Europe.

They left behind ugly buildings in countryside quiet once more, some to rot and others to find agricultural use; concrete runways and roads to obstruct the plough - and accounts of who they were and what they did which tend to become increasingly inaccurate with time.

This short narrative can give little impression of life within the perimeters, but it may perhaps help to prevent legend becoming myth.

We are indebted to the Imperial War Museum for permission to reproduce the photographs in this publication.